Fleet Street Eclogues (Second Series) by John Davidson

John Davidson was born at Barrhead, East Renfrewshire on 11th April 1857.

In 1862 his family moved to Greenock and there he began his education at Highlanders' Academy. Davidson would now spend many years at school and the beginnings of a career in various industries before gaining employment in various schools.

By now literature was a large part of his activities and his first published work was 'Bruce, A Chronicle Play' in 1886. Four other plays quickly followed including the somewhat brilliant pantomimic 'Scaramouch in Naxos' (1889).

With his reputation gradually providing an income he was also able to explore his true medium; Verse. 'In a Music Hall and Other Poems' (1891) together with 'Fleet Street Eclogues' (1893) were ample proof that he possessed a quite rare, genuine and distinctive poetic gift.

Davidson now turned further and further towards verse. In 1894 he published his most popular volume, 'Ballads and Songs' (1894), and this was followed by a further 'Fleet Street Eclogues' (Second Series) (1896) and by 'New Ballads' (1897) and 'The Last Ballad' (1899).

As the new century dawned Davidson was hard at work on a series of 'Testaments', in which he gave definite expression to his philosophy and were published over a seven year period; 'The Testament of a Vivisector' (1901), 'The Testament of a Man Forbid' (1901), 'The Testament of an Empire Builder' (1902), and 'The Testament of John Davidson' (1908).

However, on 23rd March 1909, with his finances in ruins, the onset of cancer and profound hopelessness and clinical depression he left his house for the last time. His body was only found on September 18th by some local fishermen.

Index of Contents

ALL HALLOW'S EVE

Basil, Menzies, Brian, Percy

Brian
Tearfully sinks the pallid sun.

Menzies

Bring in the lamps: Autumn is done.

Percy

Nay, twilight silvers the flashing drops;
And a whiter fall is behind.

Brian

And the wild east mouths the chimney-tops,
The Pandean pipes of the wind.

Menzies

The dripping ivy drapes the walls;
The drenched red creepers flare;
And the draggled chestnut plumage falls
In every park and square.

Percy

Nay, golden garlands strew the way
For the old triumph of decay.

Basil

And I know, in a living land of spells —
In an excellent land of rest,
Where a crimson fount of sunset wells
Out of the darkling west —
That the poplar, the willow, the scented lime,
Full-leaved in the shining air
Tarry as if the enchanter time
Had fixed them deathless there.
In arbours and noble palaces
A gallant people live
With every manner of happiness
The amplest life can give.

Percy

Where? where? In Elfland?

Menzies

No; oh no!

In Elfland is no rest,
But rumour and stir and endless woe
Of the unfulfilled behest —
The doleful yoke of the Elfin folk
Since first the sun went west.

The cates they eat and the wine they drink,
Savourless nothings are;
The hopes they cherish, the thoughts they think
Are neither near nor far;
And well they know they cannot go
Even to a desert star:

One planet is all their poor estate,
Though a million systems roll;
They are dogged and worried, early and late,
As the demons nag a soul,
By the moon and the sun, for they never can shun
Time's tyrannous control.

The haughty delicate style they keep
Only the blind can see;
On holy nights in the forest deep.
When they make high revelry
Under the moon, the dancing tune
Is the wind in a Cypress tree.

They burn the elfin midnight oil
Over their tedious lore;
They spin the sand; and still they toil
Though their inmost hearts are sore —
The doleful yoke of the restless folk
For ever and ever more.

But could you capture the elfin queen
Who once was Caesar's prize,
Daunt and gyve her with glances keen
Of unimpassioned eyes,
And hear unstirred her magic word,
And scorn her tears and sighs,

Lean would she seem at once, and old;
Her rosy mouth decayed;
Her heavy tresses of living gold,
All withered in the braid;
In your very sight the dew and the light
Of her eyes would parch and fade;

And she, the immortal phantom dame,
Would vanish from your ken;
For the fate of the elves is nearly the same
As the terrible fate of men:
To love; to rue: to be and pursue
A flickering wisp of the fen.

We must play the game with a careless smile,
Though there's nothing in the hand;
We must toil as if it were worth our while
Spinning our ropes of sand;
And laugh and cry, and live and die
At the waft of an unseen wand.

But the elves, besides the endless woe
Of the unfulfilled behest,
Have only a phantom life, and so
They neither can die nor rest —
Have no real being at all, and know
That therefore they never can rest —
The doleful yoke of the deathless folk
Since first the sun went west.

Percy
Then where is the wonderful land of spells,
Where a crimson fount of sunset wells,
And the poplar, the willow, the scented lime
Tarry, full-leaved, till the winter-time.
Where endless happiness life can give.
And only heroic people live?

Basil
We know, we know, we spinners of sand!
In the heart of the world is that gracious land;
And it never can fade while the sap returns,
While the sun gives light, and the red blood burns.

LAMMAS

Herbert, Percy, Sandy, Ninian

Percy
A health, in cider, golden, racy, rough —
The harvest and the harvesters!

Sandy
I drink
In amber spirit that enshrines the heart
Of an old Lothian summer.

Percy
Summers old

And Gules of August! — to their memory
I drink, and to the memory of those
Who wielded shining sickles. Forth they went,
The gaunt and ragged heralds of the morn:
Before them spread the sighing leagues of grain;
Behind, the tardy sun arose and struck
All day on men and women obstinate
Against the stubborn ranks, the golden horde:
Silent and set, as their long-sworded sires
Who fought the crashing rollers on the strand
And stared athwart the ocean wistfully
Into the moaning storm, the reapers reaped:
And they grew lean; and the sun burnt them black:

A sea of living gold poured round their feet
And rose in crested shocks; still and anon
The whetstone shrieked against the curving blade.
I drink the swarthy harvesters of old!

Herbert
To them all honour I But I also drink
The merry singing wheels that lighten toil.

Sandy
And drive men into cities where they rot!
Nor do they lighten toil —

Ninian
A truce to this!
Let us see things and say them. Why debate?

Sandy
Debate? The sergeant-major of the tongue!
Rather we should invite his discipline.

Percy
Well said, indeed! It is this same Debate
That overmasters armies; that distils
From rancorous commotion amity;
It is the proof, sifter and alkahest
Of all opinion, and the ordeal keen
Of knowledge, reason and intelligence;
The arbiter of right; the only source,
Camp, castle and estate of liberty.
The sword did never yet perpetuate
The work it reared — too sharp a trowel, still
With bloody mortar building on the sand
The word alone endures; but prophecy

Being now invalid, we exalt Debate.

Sandy
The blare of personal and party aims
In parliaments and journals seems indeed
No substitute for Sinai; but it serves:
And from the vehement logomachy
Of interest and cabal, something humane
At happy intervals proceeds.

Ninian
How now!
'Something humane at happy intervals!'
A meagre output for your demiurge!

Percy
Debate, like every energy divine,
Careless of centuries, elaborates
Events effectual for eternity.
The cavillers, impatient of delay.
Like little boys that violate the earth
To see if seedlings sprout, resent the mode,
When they descry the immaterial
Advancement in a decade; but we know.
We, ponderers devout of secular years.
How this most tedious Cyclops, this Debate,
Laborious long in darkness and distress,
Hammered and forged the adamantine chains
That shackle tyranny, and now begins
To smelt the ore from which shall yet be wrought
A kingly crown for every child of man.

Ninian
I see no hope in wrangling. Nations pass
From panic into panic; all men seem
Fools or fanatics.

Percy
Well? . . . Proceed; discuss.

Ninian
Not I; for now you put me on my guard
Sometimes when I forget myself I talk
As though I were persuaded of the truth
Of some received or unreceived belief;
But always afterwards I am ashamed
Of such lewd lapses into bigotry.

Percy
Intolerantly tolerant, I say!

Sandy
This is debauchery: defend yourself!

Ninian
I cannot; I have tried it many a time,
And always foiled, because the thing I say
Seems not more just than that which I deny;
Nor would I if I could, because to me
It now appears inept to take a side.
I know that silence would become me best,
And I endeavour to be quiet.

Sandy
Oh!

Ninian
Indeed I do. . . . Now I shall say no more.

Herbert
Why do you take offence so readily?

Ninian
I am not well: I am haunted. Lo, I stand
On Arthur's Seat. 'The chill and brindled fog
That plumed the Bass and belted Berwick Law,
That hung with ghostly tapestry the stones
Of bleak Tantallon, from the windy Forth,
Noiseless and dim, speeds by the pier of Leith,
And by Leith Walk, its dreary channel old,
To flood the famous city, Edinburgh.
Then, like the spectre of an inland sea
By wanton sorcerers troubled and destroyed.
It foams with whitening surges through the vale,
The fair green hollow over Salisbury Crags;
And rises clasping every gentle slope,
Uneven scar, and fairy-girdled knoll.
Till with the hungry passion of the dead
It hugs the high earth, frantic to supply
Its own lean misty ribs, and live again
Terrestrial, with the mountain for a soul.
I stand and watch. The fog begins to ebb;
And sunset weaves of all the waning wreaths
A veil of lace, investing goldenly
The rock-piled castle — plinth and monolith
Of ruby deep and dark in soaring groups;

The Monument aflame with chrysolite;
St Giles's garland-crown studded with gems.
A bell rings faintly: curled and braided smoke
O'erhangs the humming Canongate, and flings
Dusky festoons that wither as they fall
About the wasted towers of Hol3n'ood.
In front the burnished disc of day descends
The ample crimson west; behind, the night
In silent legions troops into the air. —
Masses of vision overwhelm me thus:
I am haunted by the heavens and the earth —
Darkness and light; and when I am addressed
I answer from the point, or petulantly,
Or say the opposite of what I would,
And am most awkward, helpless, and forlorn.
Wherefore I shun the company of men.
Not fearing them, but fearful of myself;
Surely to strive to please and still to fail
Is to be wretched in the last degree.

Sandy
Then do not strive to please: contemn contempt.
And trust yourself.

Ninian
But I mistrust myself:
A word, a glance, a cloud, a beam of light,
A perfume from its orbit shakes my soul.

Sandy
This weakness comes because you look without.

Ninian
I look without: you look within: what then?
You are possessed; I, obsessed: that is all.
I am besieged by things that I have seen:
Followed and watched by rivers; snared and held
In lab3nrinthine woods and tangled meads;
Hemmed in by mountains; waylaid.by the sun;
Environed and beset by moon and stars;
Whispered by winds and summoned by the sea.

Herbert
What do you note now?

Ninian
By a Kentish road,
Across the down where poles in ricks repose,

Delivered from the burden of the bines,
And golden apples on their twisted boughs
Illumine ancient orchards, descend,
Watching and wondering to the Medway's bank.
The alder and the hazel dip their leaves;
The grass-green willow shakes; the spiny thorn,
Embossed and lustrous with its load of haws,
Shines in the water like a burning bush:
And broad and deep, muttering outlandish things,
The heavy river rolls its umber flood.
Convolvuluses overhang the brink,
Pallid or watchet-hued, and still as bells
That in a trance imagine tuneful chimes
Of virtue to enchant a moonlit mere.
On river lawns with emerald velvet spread
The ewes sedately browse the three-piled nap.
A distant clang of shouts and laughter rings
Across the valley from the gleaming terts
Of sunburnt hoppers at their evening meal;
And fainter voices from the roadside inn
Echo about the air, and dwell and die.
Crowned by the yellow oasthouse from whose cowl
Banners and scarfs of fleecy smoke hang out,
And busked with serried, tawny-clustered vines.
Far-reaching slopes lean up along the sky.
The drowsy wind touches a fitful stop;
The Medway mutters dreaming as it rolls;
In bronzing brakes and thickets deeply choired
Autumnal tokens birds at leisure pipe;
While the sun, shut within a donjon high
Of massive cloud, through secret loopholes flings
His moted beams that quiver visibly
Broadcast; or seem ethereal lances, stacked
By the celestial watchmen who patrol
The world at night, and on their silent rounds
Move to the ghostly music of the spheres.

Herbert
And whence comes this obsession?

Ninian
Hark! Behold!
The floor is flooded with the tide. I lounge
Upon a shingle bolster. Dimly seen
Beyond the weathergleam a pennon'd mast,
A drift of smoke, hover and disappear;
And in the midst dark sails of mackerel boats
Over a reach of water, brown as tan,

Dance, deftly tripping the uneven waves.
Nearer, a yellow width unwinds; between,
A point of emerald glows, and suddenly
Shoots out and bums its way towards the west —
A spark in tinder, then a stripe of fire.
And last a sheet of phosphorescent green
Fuming with white waves. Listen! at my feet
The uplifted shuddering rollers headlong fell.
And jangle on the beach as the surf breaks
In silver chains and shekels; while the wind
Out of the southwest sings across the deep.
Straightway a new sky makes another sea.
Occultly gifted, light upon the waves
Juggles with hidden beams behind a cloud
Bright but impenetrable. Near the shore
A vein of saffron shines; beyond, a band
Of olive hue blends with a sapphire zone;
Further away, wine-coloured water heaves
Against a high sea-wall of swarthy fog.
Is it the sea that gleams in merging breadths
Of colour dark and wet? Or do the powers,
That decorate the quarters of the world,
In some vast crucible dissolve and fuse
Virginal mines of ruby, malachite,
Jacinth and chrysoprase to pave the floor
Of ocean rough with wrecks and skeletons?
Nature is now about some mystery!
But while I watch, ere I can mark the change,
The passionate sun flames through the shrivelled cloud.
And all the crisp and curling water wakes,
Blue as the naked sky that bathes in it.

Herbert
How does it happen you are so beset?

Ninian
I shall attempt to tell you honestly.
It was engraven deeply on my mind
In daily lessons from my infancy
Until I left my father's house, that not
Ability and knowledge, beauty and strength,
But goodness only can avail. I watched.
And thought I understood that beauty, strength
And knowledge ought to reign, they being indeed
The trinity of goodness; but I claimed
That this should be revealed to me, that I
Should be directly warned by God Himself
In the old fashion. Strange it seems; and yet

It was not very strange. Each mom and eve,
Year after year, I heard the prophets read,
Heard strong believing prayer: the atmosphere
Was not allied more nearly to my breath
Than to my mind the thought of God — no dream
Of deity; a living, active God.
On hill-tops, by the sea, in storm, in calm
I cried to Him to speak to me; with tears
Solicited a sign. Sleepless and pale
I wandered like a ghost, and day and night
Waited upon a message from on high.
Sunset and sunrise came; the seasons past;
The years went slowly by; but still to me
The universe was dumb. Books helped me not,
Except for pleasure or to gain command
Of words: I would have God's own voice or none
At last I ceased to hope and found content
In roaming through the land. The magic sun
Drew pictures on my sight. Wondering I watched;
Nor could the secular fairy ever change
My wonder into curiosity.
All my emotion and imagining
Were of the finest tissue that is woven
From sense and thought. No well-thumbed page appeared
In the hard book of memory when I woke:
Amazed I trembled newly into life:
I seemed to be created every morn.
A golden trumpet pealed along the sky:
The sun arose; the whole earth rushed upon me.
Sometimes the tree that stroked my window-pane
Was more than I could grasp; sometimes my thought
Absorbed the universe, which fell away
And dwindled from my ken, as if my mind
Had been the roomy continent of space. —
My way of life led me to London town,
And difficulties — which I overcame.
Equipped with patience and necessity.
Then suddenly before my thoughts might leap
Resurgent from the living tomb of care
And dip their wings in dawn, about me clung
The slimy folds of sin: its nether coils
Are hidden in the sepulchre of time,
The glutted past; the pallid future strains
In travail with its fiery eyes and fangs:
I peer from out the slippery middle wreaths
And see blurred visions of the world, or watch
The flashing scenes that haunt my memory.
When heedfully I viewed my latter days —

Considering for the first time in my life
The naked facts of my affairs and me —
I found that underneath indifference
To every aim saving a livelihood
And leisure to enjoy nature and art.
My source of strength, though never to myself
Confessed before, had been the lurking thought
That poison, or a bullet, or the waves
Could stop the unendurable ecstasy
Of pain or pleasure, at whichever pole
Of passion I determined to forsake
The orb of life, on my acceptance thrust
In ignorance and disregard of me.
My temperament and fitness for the gift;
But now that refuge of despair is shut.
For other lives have twined themselves with mine.
And yet. . . . How shall I seize you with due dread
Of the offensive tide that stifles me,
The worm obscene in whose close coils I writhe? . . .
Now I conceive it clearly; you shall mark
Fate's way with me! A tedious decade hence
My son shall come and pitifully cry,

'Father, why am I weak, outclassed, outcast?
'I cannot do the things that others do;
'I take no place in work or play; my brains
'Are unelastic: something in my head
'Snaps when I fain would study; visions rise
'Unsummoned; phantom tongues mumble strange news;
'And when I would contend in games, my bones
'Grow pithless, and my sinews shrink; my heart! —
'Who wore it out with sensual drudgery
'Before it came to me? what warped its valves?
'It has been used: my heart is secondhand!
'Why had I not the force to be born great,
'Fit for a splendid stage, a noble part,
'A crisis in the world? Why must I think
'Such things at seventeen? Why think at all
'When love should lap me in a constant dream?
'I have no faith instinctive in myself;
'No reservoir profound of energy;
'No fathomless resource; no central fire;
'No passionate aroma in my blood
'Filling the world with fragrance where I come;
'No rapt imagination to transmute
'All pallor into glory. Life you gave:
'Where is my birthright, sir, beauty and strength?'
What can I say to him?

Herbert, Percy, Sandy
The truth!

Ninian
This then:—
'My son, your ancestors supplanted you:
'You are my child; hence are your teeth on edge.
'Our blood is stale; the tree from which we spring
'Fades at the top. Two of our family
'Have died insane in my time: one I saw
'Go mad. The sounds and sights that visit you
'Attend me too, foretellers of our doom.
'The ultimate iniquity is mine;
'But from a root in distant ages sunk
'The loathsome filaments entangle you.
'And I impeach the smooth conniving world,
'The bland accomplice that has made and makes
'A merit of defect, a cult of woe,
'Sowing exhausted land with seed that's foul,
'To harvest tares of madness, impotence,
'Uncomeliness in wasteful granaries —
'I mean asylums, prisons, hospitals.
'If only nineteen hundred years ago
'A gospel of the pride of life had rung
'Our doleful era in; if the device
'In nature's choice of beauty and of strength
'Had then been shown to man, how had the world
'Approved the excellent expedient,
'With voluntary euthanasia
'Weeded humanity at once, and made
'A race of heroes in a golden age! . . .
'This helps not. All the blame is mine, my son,
'Who never should have been' ... It palsies me;
I cannot comfort him; he stands and stares
Defeated ere he was begot. — Behold
The ancient snake that pinions me! Like one
Chained to a column in a turbid stream.
About my ears a sluggish billow flaps,
And chokes and daubs me with its ropy wash.

Sandy
Escape! I know the manner! Live at speed;
And call your least caprice the law of God;
Disdain the shows of things, and every love
Whose stamen is not hate; self-centred stand;
Accept no second thought; in every throb
Your heart gives, every murmur of your mind,

Listen devoutly to the trump of doom.
You are your birthright; let it serve you well:
Be your own star, for strength is from within,
And one against the world will always win!

Ninian
I cannot act. The subtle coils grow tense.
And crush my limbs, my heart, my throat, my head.
I am the sufferer, the endurer, I.
Yet God who gives no presage hitherto,
Haply intends hereafter to be heard.
I am not thinking solely of myself,
But of the groaning cataract of life,
The ruddy stream that leaps importunate
Out of the night, and in a moment vaults
The immediate treacherous precipice of time.
Splashing the stars, downward into the night.
Meanwhile for me no lulling opiate,
No dream, no mystic solvent: I must watch
Hopeless, unhelped, till I go mad or die.

Herbert
But you have hope and help.

Ninian
I? Show me them!

Herbert
You went forth seeking God and found the world
The sounds and sights that haunt, and help and please.
The canopy and state of day and night:
The pageant of the year; the changing moods,
The loyal constancy and testament
Of Nature — her asides, her hints, and smiles,
Her clear ideas of repose and toil.
Her covenant and noble ministry
Of light and darkness, and of life and death.
Are the true salve for your distempered mind.
Blame not yourself too much; admit no fear
Of madness with the sunrise in your blood;
And hold your own intelligence in awe
As the most high: there is no other God —
No God at all; yet God is in the womb —
A living God, no mystic deity.
With idols in its infancy the world
Deceived itself as maidens do with dolls.
And as it grew pretended and believed
That what it should bring forth already reigned.

Now is its hour come, but it only knows
The sick dismay and anguish, ignorant
Of birth-pangs and an offspring more divine
Than man has yet imagined. I have woes,
As you and all men have in their degree;
So let us think we are the tortured nerves
Of Being in travail with a higher type.
I know that I shall crumble back to dust,
And cease for evermore from sense and thought,
But this contents me well in my distress: —
I, being human, touch the highest reach
Attained by matter, and within me feel
The motion of a loftier than I:
Out of the beast came man; from man comes God.
Deepest delight is in the certainty
That to the all pervading element
Wherein the universe disports a while,
Ethereal oblivion, my deeds
And I eternally belong.

Ninian
Yes . . . See,
They throng the room! — no spectres, but themselves:
Sibilant depths of darkness; avenues
Of latticed light; ambrosial, pine-strewn glades;
Ravines and waterfalls; the grass-green turf.
Where primroses by secret alchemy
Distil from buried treasure golden leaves,
And where forget-me-nots above the tombs
Of snow-drops hang their candelabra, trimmed
With azure light — turquoise by magic roots
Drawn from the bowels of the earth and changed
To living flame; roses, laburnum, lilac;
Sunrise and sunset like a glowing vice
Bloodstained that grips the world; the restless moon
Swung low to light us; clouds; the limpid sky;
The bourdon of the great ground-bee, athwart
A lonely hill-side, vibrant on the air.
And subtler than the scent of violets;
Sonorous winds, storm, thunder, and the sea.

MIDSUMMER DAY

Basil, Sandy, Herbert

Sandy

I cannot write, I cannot think;
'Tis half delight and half distress:
My memory stumbles on the brink
Of some unfathomed happiness —

Of some old happiness divine.
What haunting scent, what haunting note,
What word, or what melodious line.
Sends my heart throbbing to my throat?

Basil
What? thrilled with happiness to-day,
The longest day in all the year,
Which we must spend in making hay
By thrashing straw in Fleet Street here!

What scent? what sound? The odour stale
Of watered streets; the bruit loud
Of hoof and wheel on road and rail.
The rush and trample of the crowd!

Herbert
Humming the song of many a lark,
Out of the sea, across the shires.
The west wind blows about the park.
And faintly stirs the Fleet Street wires.

Perhaps it sows the happy seed
That blossoms in your memory;
Certain of many a western mead,
And hill and stream it speaks to me.

With rosy showers of apple-bloom
The orchard sward is mantled deep;
Shaded in some sequestered coombe
The red deer in the Quantocks sleep.

Basil
Go on: of rustic visions tell
Till I forget the wilderness
Of sooty brick, the dusty smell,
The jangle of the printing-press.

Herbert
I hear the woodman's measured stroke;
I see the amber streamlet glide —
Above, the green gold of the oak
Fledges the gorge on either side.

A thatched roof shines athwart the gloom
Of the high moorland's darksome ground;
Far off the surging rollers boom,
And fill the shadowy wood with sound

Basil
You have pronounced the magic sign!
The city with its thousand years,
Like some embodied mood of mine
Uncouth, prodigious, disappears.

I stand upon a lowly bridge.
Moss-grown beside the old Essex home;
Over the distant purple ridge
The clouds arise in sultry foam;

In many a cluster, wreath and chain
A silvery vapour hangs on high,
And snowy scarfs of silken grain
Bedeck the blue slopes of the sky;

The wandering water sighs and calls,
And breaks into a chant that rings
Beneath the vaulted bridge, then falls
And under heaven softly sings;

A light wind lingers here and there.
And whispers in an unknown tongue
The passionate secrets of the air,
That never may by men be sung:

Low, low, it whispers; stays, and goes;
It comes again; again takes flight;
And like a subtle presence grows
And almost gathers into sight.

Sandy
The wind that stirs the Fleet Street wires,
And roams and quests about the Park,
That wanders all across the shires.
Humming the song of many a lark —

The wind — it is the wind, whose breath.
Perfumed with roses, wakes in me
From shrouded slumbers deep as death
A yet unfaded memory.

Basil
About Midsummer, every hour
Ten thousand rosebuds opening blush,
The land is all one rosy bower.
And rosy odours haunt and flush

The winds of heaven up and down:
On the top-gallant of the air
The lark, the pressman in the town
Breathe only rosy incense rare.

Sandy
And I, enchanted by the rose.
Remember when I first began
To know what in its bosom glows
Exhaling scent ambrosian.

A child, at home in streets and quays,
The city tumult in my brain,
I only knew of tarnished trees.
And skies corroding vapours stain.

One summer — Time upon my head
Had showered the curls of years eleven—
Me, for a month, good fortune led
Where trees are green and hills kiss heaven.

By glen and mountain, moor and lawn,
Bum-side and sheep-path, day and night,
I wandered, a belated faun,
All sense, all wonder, all delight.

And once at eve I climbed a hill.
Burning to see the sun appear,
And watched the jewelled darkness fill
With lamps and clustered tapers clear.

At last the strongest stars were spent;
A glimmering shadow overcame
The swarthy-purple firmament.
And throbbed and kindled into flame;

The pallid day, the trembling day
Put on her saffron wedding-dress,
And watched her bridegroom far away
Soar through the starry wilderness.

I clasped my hands and closed my eyes,

And tears relieved my ecstasy:
T dared not watch the sun arise;
Nor knew what magic daunted me:

And yet the roses seemed to tell
More than the mom, had I but known
The meaning of the fragrant smell
That bound me with a subtle zone.

But in the gloaming when we played
At hide-and-seek, and I with her
Behind a rose-bush hid, afraid
To meet her gaze, to breathe, or stir,

The dungeon of my sense was riven,
The beauty of the world laid bare,
A great wind caught me up to heaven
Upon a cloud of golden hair;

And mouth touched mouth; and love was born;
And when our wondering vision blent,
We found the meaning of the morn,
The meaning of the rose's scent.

Ah me! ah me! since then I since then!

Herbert
Nay, nay; let self-reproaches be!
Now that this thought is throned again,
Be zealous for its sovereignty.

Basil
And brave, great Nature must be thanked;
And we must worship on our knees,
And hold for ever sacro-sanct
Such dewy memories as these.

MAYDAY

Brian, Menzies

Brian
Late — you are late. And where have you been?

Menzies
I have been in the woods and the lanes.

Brian
And what have you heard, and what have you seen,
And what in your fancy reigns?

Menzies
I have heard the ring-dove coo,
And the cuckoo toll his bell;
I have seen the shrieking jay flash blue
Athwart a wooded dell.
I have heard the chattering streamlet run
In haste to reach the sea;

I have watched the golden bee,
Cupid and Hymen in one,
Morn, noon, and afternoon.
Fulfil the tingling hours
With the murmuring sound of his bridal tune
As he married the waiting flowers.

The long, long hedgerows white with May
Bordered the rustling lanes;
And a fragrant wind blew all the day.

Brian
But what in your fancy reigns?

Menzies
There reigned, and is regnant still,
A memory, long forgot.
Of a lowland town, a lowland hill.
And a lowland woman's lot.

She shed her tears, and dreamed her dreams,
And wore her sad wan smiles.
Where a wide water winds and gleams
Among its links and isles.

Rock-perched a royal borough towers
High over the highest trees.
With crumbling walls and faded bowers
And mouldering palaces.

Near by a hill its dark crest lifts
Sheer from the river bank.
And cloudy shadow broods and shifts
About its russet flank.

The land is stained with purple dyes
Of high-romantic scenes;
The air still quivers with the sighs
Of tragic kings and queens;

The very ploughman holds his plough
As proudly as a lance;
The milkmaid bears a dreamy brow,
Inheriting romance.

Even in my father's time a crew
Of lads and lasses gay
Would dip their faces in the dew
Upon the first of May.

This joyful mood might not withstand
The age's growing care,
When railways hacked and scored the land,
And wires engraved the air.

One woman only, all forlorn.
While twenty summers flew,
Still climbed the hill each May-day morn
Her beauty to renew!

What love, what loss, what hope was hers
No man or maid could tell.
But all the loyal lowlanders
Esteemed her custom well.

Dressed in a hat with broken plume,
A cape, and worn black frock.
Before the dawn she left her room,
And climbed by scar and rock.

And so to-day by lane and burn,
By scented hedge and shaw,
At many a pause and sudden turn
Her wistful face I saw.

And once as in a waking dream
The whole fair lowland shone —
The palaced rock, the hill, the stream,
The softly coming dawn:

And she with sobs and murmured cries
To earth's green bosom laid
Her withered cheek, while from her eyes

Hot dew on cold dew strayed.

Brian
What was her end?

Menzies
Oh, exquisite!
Winter and Spring she lay
Bedridden in a palsy fit;
But on the first of May,

When the lark waked the sun, she too
Arose, and in a trance
Went forth to bathe her face in dew,
The martyr of romance.

They found her on the green hill-side
At home, and sleeping fast
Her endless sleep, Death's pallid bride.
Most beautiful at last.

(Singing within)

'Remember us poor Mayers ally
'And thus we do begin
'To had our lives in righteousness,
'Or else we die in sin.
'I have been rambling all this nighty
'And almost all this day,
'And now returned back again
'I bring you a branch of May.'

Brian
An antique minstrel! Hark!

Menzies
It is Basil: I know his note.

[Enter **Basil**, carrying a branch of hawthorn blossom.

Menzies
Have you been where the night-jar haunts the dark
In outland ways remote?

Basil
I have been with the nightingale:
I have learned his song so sweet:
I sang it aloud by wood and dale,

And under my breath in the street.
If the words would only flow —

Menzies
Oh, sing it now!

Basil
No, no!
But it went like this, I think: —

'Where the purple hyacinths grew,
'And the campions white ahd pink,
'The jewelled butterflies flew
'From jewelled cups to drink;
'And some were violet-eyed,
'Some blue, some rosy-red,
'Gold-plumed, or damask-dyed,
'Earth-born and heaven-bred;
'And every chalice drooped and sighed
'When the splendid revellers fled;
'But never a flower its cup denied
'Though the wine of life was shed.

'The lark from the top of heaven raved
'Of the sunshine sweet and old;
'And the whispering branches dipped and laved
'In the light; and waste and wold
'Took heart and shone; and the buttercups paved
'The emerald meads with gold«
'Now in the forest is night;
'The flowers have gone to sleep;
'But the stars have opened their eyes of light
'Under the brows of heaven deep;
'And gentle shadows cross my sight,
'And murmurs rustle and creep;
'And the very darkness is fresh and bright
'With the tears the sweet dews weep.

'The wind steals down the lawns
'With a whisper of ecstasy,
'Of moonlit nights and rosy dawns,
'And a nest in a hawthorn tree,
'Of the little mate for whom I wait,
'Flying across the sea,
'Through storm and night as sure as fate,
'Swift-winged with love for me.'

Menzies

And so you brought home the May
With the nightingale's song in your ears.

Basil
And sad eyes flashed for a moment gay,
Or welled with happy tears,
When they saw my branch and remembered the day,
And forgot the tedious years.
And thought as I tuned my rhyme,
And waved the branch in my hand,
Of the famous olden time
When a Maypole stood in the Strand.

Brian
Let the Golden Days return!

Menzies
And let the May-Queen reign!

Basil
When smokeless fires burn,
And London is born again!

ST GEORGE'S DAY

Basil, Menzies, Percy, Brian, Herbert, Sandy

Herbert
I hear the lark and linnet sing;
I hear the whitethroat's alto ring,

Menzies
I hear the idle workman sigh;
I hear his hungry children cry.

Sandy
Still sad and brooding over ill:
Why listen to discordant tones?

Herbert
We dream, we sing, we drive the quill
To keep the flesh upon our bones.
Therefore what trade have we with wrongs,
With ways and woes that spoil our songs?

Menzies

None, none! Alas, there lies the sting!
We see, we feel, but cannot aid;
We hide our foolish heads and sing:
We live, we die; and all is said.

Herbert
To wonder-worlds of old romance
Our aching thoughts for solace run.

Brian
And some have stolen fire from France.

Sandy
And some adore the Midnight sun.

Menzies
I, too, for light the world explore,
And trembling, tread where angels trod;
Devout at every shrine adore,
And follow after each new god.
But by the altar everywhere
I find the money-changer's stall;
And littering every temple-stair
The sick and sore like maggots crawl.

Basil
Your talk is vain; your voice is hoarse.

Menzies
I would they were as hoarse and vain
As their wide-weltering spring and source
Of helpless woe, of wrath insane.

Herbert
Why will you hug the coast of Hell?

Brian
Why antedate the Judgment Day?

Menzies
Nay, flout me not; you know me well.

Basil
Right, comrade! Give your fancy way.

Menzies
I cannot see the stars and flowers,
Nor hear the lark's soprano ring.

Because a ruddy darkness lowers
For ever, and the tempests sing.
I see the strong coerce the weak,
And labour overwrought rebel;
I hear the useless treadmill creak,
The prisoner, cursing in his cell;
I see the loafer-burnished wall;
I hear the rotting match-girl whine;
I see the unslept switchman fall;
I hear the explosion in the mine;
I see along the heedless street
The sandwichmen trudge through the mire;
I hear the tired quick tripping feet
Of sad, gay girls who ply for hire.

Basil
To brood on feeble woe at length
Must drive the sanest thinker mad;
Consider rather weal and strength.

Menzies
On what foundations do they stand?
I mark the sable ironclad
In every sea; in every land,
An army, idling on the chain
Of rusty peace that chafes and frets
Its seven-leagued limbs, and bristled mane
Of glittering bayonets;
The glowing blast, the fire-shot smoke
Where guns are forged and armour-plate;
The mammoth hammer's pounding stroke;
The din of our dread iron date.
And always divers undertones
Within the roaring tempest throb—
The chink of gold, the labourer's groans,
The infant's wail, the woman's sob.
Hoarsely they beg of Fate to give
A little lightening of their woe,
A little time to love, to live,
A little time to think and know.
I see where from the slums may rise
Some unexpected dreadful dawn —
The gleam of steeled and scowling eyes,
A flash of women's faces wan!

Basil
This is St George's Day.

Menzies

St George? A wretched thief I vow.

Herbert

Nay, Menzies, you should rather say,
St George for Merry England, now!

Sandy

That surely is a phantom cry,
Hollow and vain for many years.

Menzies

I hear the idle workmen sigh;
I hear the drip of women's tears.

Herbert

I hear the lofty lark,
The lowly nightingale

Basil

The Present is a dungeon dark
Of social problems. Break the gcal!
Get out into the splendid Past
Or bid the splendid Future hail.

Menzies

Nor then, nor now, nor first, nor last,
I know. The slave of ruthless Law,
To me Time seems a dungeon vast
Where Life lies rotting in the straw.

Basil

I care not for your images
Of Life and Law. I want to sing
Of England and of Englishmen
Who made our country what it is.

Herbert

And I to praise the English Spring.

Percy

St George for Merry England, then!

Menzies

There is no England now, I fear.

Basil

No England, say you, and since when?

Menzies

Cockney and Celt and Scot are here,
And Democrats and ' ans ' and ' ists '
In dubs and cliques and divers lists;
But now we have no Englishmen.

Basil

You utter what you never felt,
I know. By bog and mount and fen,
No Saxon, Norman, Scot, or Celt
I find, but only Englishmen.

Herbert

In all our hedges roses bud.

Basil

And thought and speech are more than blood.

Herbert

Away with spleen, and let us sing
The praises of the English Spring I

Basil

In weeds of gold and purple hues
Glad April bursts with piping news
Of swifts and swallows come again,
And of the tender pensive strain
The bulfinch sings from bush to bush.

Percy

And oh! the blackbird and the thrush
Interpret as no master may
The meaning of the night and day.

Sandy

They catch the whispers of the breeze
And weave them into melodies.

Brian

They utter for the hours that pass
The purpose of their moments bright.

Basil

They speak the passion of the grass,
That grows so stoutly day and night.

Herbert

St George for merry England then!
For we are all good Englishmen I

Percy
We stand as our forefathers stood
For Liberty's and Conscience' sake.

Herbert
We are the sons of Robin Hood,
The sons of Hereward the Wake.

Percy
The sons of yeomen, English-fed,
Ready to feast or drink or fight.

Herbert
The sons of kings — of Hal and Ned,
Who kept their island right and tight.

Percy
The sons of Cromwell's Ironsides,
Who knew no king but God above.

Basil
We are the sons of English brides.
Who married Englishmen for love.

Sandy
Oh, now I see Fate's means and ends!
The Bruce and Wallace wight I ken,
Who saved old Scotland from its friends,
Were mighty northern Englishmen.

Brian
And Parnell, who so greatly fought
Against a wanton useless yoke.
With Fate inevitably wrought
That Irish should be English folk.

Basil
By bogland, highland, down, and fen.
All Englishmen, all Englishmen!

Menzies
There is no England now, I say —

Brian
No England now! My grief, my grief!

Menzies
We lie widespread, the dragon-prey
Of any Cappadocian thief.
In Arctic and Pacific seas
We lounge and loaf: and either pole
We reach with sprawling colonies —
Unwieldy limbs that lack a soul.

Basil
St George for Greater England, then!
The Boreal and the Austral men!
They reverence the heroic roll
Of Englishmen who sang and fought:
They have a soul, a mighty soul,
The soul of English speech and thought.

Sandy
And when the soul of England slept —

Basil
St George for foolish England, then! —

Sandy
Lo! Washington and Lincoln kept
America for Englishmen!

Basil
Hurrah! The English people reigns
Across the wide Atlantic flood!
It could not bind itself in chains!
For Yankee blood is English blood.

Herbert
And here the spring is queen
In robes of white and green.

Percy
In chestnut sconces opening wide
Tapers shall bum some fresh May mom.

Brian
And the elder brightens the highway side,
And the briony binds the thorn.

Sandy
White is the snow of the leafless sloe
The saxifrage by the sedge,

And white the lady-amocks a-row
And sauce-alone in the hedge.

Basil
England is in her Spring;
She only begins to be.
Oh! for an organ voice to sing
The summer I can see!

But the Past is there; and a mole may know,
And a bat may understand,
That we are the people wherever we go —
Kings by sea and land!

Herbert
And the spring is crowned and stoled
In purple and in gold.

Percy
Wherever light, wherever shade is,
Gold and purple may be seen.

Brian
Gold and purple lords-and-ladies
Tread a measure on the green.

Herbert
In deserts where the wild wind blows
Blossoms the magic hæmony.

Percy
Deep in the Chiltern woodland glows
The purple pasque anemone.

Basil
And England still grows great
And never shall grow old;
Within our hands we hold
The world's fate.

Menzies
We hold the world's fate?
The cry seems out of date.

Basil
Not while a single Englishman
Can work with English brains and bones!
Awaiting us since time began,

The swamps of ice, the wastes of flame!
In Boreal and Austral zones
Took life and meaning when we came.
The Sphinx that watches by the Nile
Has seen great empires pass away:
The mightiest lasted but a while;
Yet ours shall not decay.
Because, although red blood may flow,
And ocean shake with shot.
Not England's sword but England's Word
Undoes the Gordian Knot.
Bold tongue, stout heart, strong hand, brave brow
The world's four quarters win;
And patiently with axe and plough
We bring the deserts in.

Menzies
Whence comes this patriotic craze?
Spare us at least the hackneyed brag
About the famous English flag.

Basil
I'll spare no flourish of its praise.
Wherever our flag floats in the wind
Order and justice dawn and shine.
The dusky myriads of Ind,
The swarthy tribes far south the line,
And all who fight with lawless law,
And all with lawless men who cope
Look hitherward across the brine,
For we are the world's forlorn hope.

Menzies
That makes my heart leap up! Hurrah!
We are the world's forlorn hope!

Herbert
And with the merry birds we sing
The praises of the English Spring.

Percy
Iris and orchis now unfold.

Brian
The drooping -leaved laburnums ope
In thunder-showers of greenish gold.

Menzies

And we are the world's forlorn hope!

Sandy
The lilacs shake their dancing plumes
Of lavender, mauve, and heliotrope.

Herbert
The speedwell on the highway blooms.

Menzies
And we are the world's forlorn hope!

Sandy
Skeletons lurk in every street.

Herbert
We push and strike for air and scope.

Brian
The pulses of rebellion beat
Where want and hunger sulk and mope.

Menzies
But though we wander far astray,
And oft in gloomy darkness grope,
Fearless we face the blackest day,
For we are the world's forlorn hope.

Sandy
St George for Merry England then!
For we are all good Englishmen!

Basil
St George for Greater England then!
The Boreal and the Austral men!

All
By bogland, highland, down, and fen,
All Englishmen, all Englishmen!
Who with their latest breath shall sing
Of England and the English Spring!

John Davidson – A Short Biography

John Davidson was born at Barrhead, East Renfrewshire on 11th April 1857, the son of Alexander Davidson, an Evangelical Union minister and Helen née Crocket of Elgin.

In 1862 the family moved to Greenock and Davidson began his education at Highlanders' Academy. From there he began his career, aged a mere 13, at the chemical laboratory of Walker's Sugarhouse refinery. A year later he returned to Highlander's, this time as a pupil teacher.

During his later employment at the Public Analysts' Office, 1870–71 he developed a keen interest in science which later became an important characteristic of his poetry. He returned once again to the Highlander's Academy, this time for four years, in 1872, again as a pupil teacher. In 1876 he spent a year at Edinburgh University before his first scholastic employment at Alexander's Charity, Glasgow which led to short periods of employment at various other schools over the following half a dozen years.

This led to a stint at Morrison's Academy in Crieff (1885–88), and in a private school at Greenock (1888–89).

In 1885 Davidson married Margaret McArthur and the marriage produced two children, Alexander (born in 1887) and Menzies (born in 1889).

Davidson's first published work was 'Bruce, A Chronicle Play', written in the Elizabethan style, and published by a local Glasgow imprint in 1886. Four other plays quickly followed; 'Smith, A Tragic Farce' (1888), 'An Unhistorical Pastoral' (1889), 'A Romantic Farce' (1889), and then the somewhat brilliant pantomime 'Scaramouch in Naxos' (1889).

By now he was very much immersed in literature and, in 1889, he ventured to London where he frequented the famous Fleet Street pub 'Ye Olde Cheshire Cheese' and joined the 'Rhymers' Club', a poets group that was based there.

Davidson was a prolific and hard-working writer. As well as his plays he wrote for the Speaker, the Glasgow Herald, and several other papers. He also wrote and had published several novels and tales, with perhaps the best being 'Perfervid' (1890).

With his reputation gradually providing an income he was also able to explore his true medium; Verse. 'In a Music Hall and Other Poems' (1891) together with 'Fleet Street Eclogues' (1893) were ample proof that he possessed a quite rare, genuine and distinctive poetic gift. Praise came from his peers including George Gissing and WB Yeats who wrote that it was: 'An example of a new writer seeking out new subject matter, new emotions'.

Davidson now turned further and further towards verse. In 1894 he published his most popular volume, 'Ballads and Songs' (1894), and this was followed by a further 'Fleet Street Eclogues' (Second Series) (1896) and by 'New Ballads' (1897) and 'The Last Ballad' (1899).

Davidson was a prolific writer. Besides the works cited, he wrote many other works including, 'The Wonderful Mission of Earl Lavender' (1895), a novel which extends his literary canon to flagellation erotica. He also contributed an introduction to Shakespeare's Sonnets (Renaissance edition, 1908), which, like his various prefaces and essays, shows him to be a subtle literary critic.

As the new century dawned Davidson was hard at work on a series of 'Testaments', in which he gave definite expression to his philosophy and these were published over a seven year period; 'The

Testament of a Vivisector' (1901), 'The Testament of a Man Forbid' (1901), 'The Testament of an Empire Builder' (1902), and 'The Testament of John Davidson' (1908).

Though he played down any thought of himself as a philosopher, he expounded an original philosophy which was at once materialistic and aristocratic.

His later verse, which is often fine rhetoric rather than poetry, expressed his belief which is summed up in the last words that he wrote, "Men are the universe become conscious; the simplest man should consider himself too great to be called after any name." Davidson professed to reject all existing philosophies, including that of Nietzsche, as inadequate. The poet planned to expand and expound on his revolutionary creed in a trilogy entitled 'God and Mammon'. Only two plays, however, were written, 'The Triumph of Mammon' (1907) and 'Mammon and his Message' (1908).

In addition to his own work Davidson was a noted translator of other works which included Montesquieu's 'Lettres Persanes' (1892), François Coppée's 'Pour la Couronne' in 1896 and Victor Hugo's 'Ruy Blas' in 1904, the former being produced as, 'For the Crown', at the Lyceum Theatre in 1896, the latter as 'A Queen's Romance' at the Imperial Theatre.

Frank Harris, a member of the Rhymers' Club and himself a writer of erotic literature described him in 1889 as: "... a little below middle height, but strongly built with square shoulders and remarkably fine face and head; the features were almost classically regular, the eyes dark brown and large, the forehead high, the hair and moustache black. His manners were perfectly frank and natural; he met everyone in the same unaffected kindly human way; I never saw a trace in him of snobbishness or incivility. Possibly a great man, I said to myself, certainly a man of genius, for simplicity of manner alone is in England almost a proof of extraordinary endowment."

In 1906 he was awarded a civil list pension of £100 per annum and George Bernard Shaw did what he could to help him financially. However other issues were also circling besides poverty. Ill-health, and his declining intellectual powers, amplified by the onset of cancer, caused profound hopelessness and clinical depression.

Late in 1908, Davidson left London to live in Penzance in Cornwall. On 23rd March 1909, he left his house and was not seen again. There seemed no sound reason not to believe that he had done so with the intention of drowning himself. On an examination of his office a new manuscript was found. It was a poetry book; 'Fleet Street Poems', with a letter bleakly stating confirming, "This will be my last book."

Indeed in his philosophic book 'The Testament of John Davidson', published the year before his death, he anticipates this fate:

"None should outlive his power. . . . Who kills
Himself subdues the conqueror of kings;
Exempt from death is he who takes his life;
My time has come."

Davidson's body was not discovered until 18th September in Mount's cave by some fishermen. In accordance with his will it was now buried at sea. Strangely it seemed Davidson's wish that none of his unpublished works, nor any biography be published and "no word except of my writing is ever to appear in any book of mine as long as the copyright endures."

Davidson's poetry was a key early influence on important Modernist poets, in particular, his compatriot Hugh MacDiarmid, Wallace Stevens and T.S. Eliot.

John Davidson – A Concise Bibliography

The North Wall (1885)
Diabolus Amans (1885) Verse drama
Bruce (1886) A drama in five acts
Smith (1888) A tragedy
An Unhistorical Pastoral, A Romantic Farce (1889)
Scaramouch in Naxos (1889)
Perfervid: The Career of Ninian Jamieson (1890) with 23 Original Illustrations by Harry Furniss
The Great Men, And a Practical Novelist (1891) Illustrated by E. J. Ellis.
In a Music Hall, and other Poems (1891)
Laura Ruthven's Widowhood (with C. J. Wills) (1892)
Fleet Street Eclogues (1893)
The Knight of the Maypole, (1903)
Sentences and Paragraphs (1893)
Ballads and Songs (1894)
Baptist Lake (1894)
A Random Itinerary (1894)
A Full and True Account of the Wonderful Mission of Earl Lavender (1895)
St. George's Day (1895)
Fleet Street Eclogues (Second Series) (1896)
Miss Armstrong's and Other Circumstances (1896)
The Pilgrimage of Strongsoul and Other Stories (1896)
New Ballads (1897)
Godfrida, a play (1898)
The Last Ballad (1899)
Self's the Man, A tragi-comedy (1901)
The Testament of a Man Forbid (1901)
The Testament of a Vivisector (1901)
The Testament of an Empire Builder (1902)
A Rosary (1903)
The Knight of the Maypole: A Comedy in Four Acts (1903)
The Testament of a Prime Minister (1904)
The Ballad of a Nun (1905)
The Theatrocrat: A Tragic Play of Church and State (1905)
Holiday and other poems, with a note on poetry (1906)
The Triumph of Mammon (1907)
Mammon and His Message (1908)
The Testament of John Davidson (1908)
Fleet Street and other Poems (1909)

He was also a contributor to 'The Yellow Book' periodical

As Translator

Montesquieu's Lettres Persanes (Persian Letters) (1892)
François Coppée's Pour la couronne (For the Crown) (1896)
Victor Hugo's Ruy Blas (A Queen's Romance) (1904)

www.ingramcontent.com/pod-product-compliance
Lightning Source LLC
Chambersburg PA
CBHW021946040426
42448CB00008B/1266